Roald Dahl

Chris Powling

Illustrated by
Stephen Gulbis

Evans Brothers Limited

For Ellie who sees herself as
R.D.'s Number One Fan

Published by Evans Brothers Limited
2A Portman Mansions
Chiltern Street
London W1M 1LE

First published in Great Britain in 1983 by
Hamish Hamilton Children's Books

© Chris Powling (text) 1983
© Stephen Gulbis (illustrations) 1983

Reprinted 1984, 1988
New edition 1993

Typeset by GCS, Leighton Buzzard, Bedfordshire

Printed in Great Britain by Ebenezer Baylis & Son Ltd,
The Trinity Press, Worcester, and London

ISBN 0 237 60010 2

Titles in this series

Ian Botham	0 237 60030 7	Bob Geldof	0 237 60031 5
Edith Cavell	0 237 60020 X	Amy Johnson	0 237 60032 3
Marie Curie	0 237 60024 2	Helen Keller	0 237 60016 1
Roald Dahl	0 237 60010 2	John F. Kennedy	0 237 60029 3
Thomas Edison	0 237 60006 4	Florence Nightingale	0 237 60018 8
Alexander Fleming	0 237 60013 7	Emmeline Pankhurst	0 237 60019 6
John Lennon	0 237 60021 8	Anna Pavlova	0 237 60002 1
Martin Luther King	0 237 60007 2	Pope John Paul II	0 237 60005 6
Nelson Mandela	0 237 60026 9	Prince Philip	0 237 60012 9
Bob Marley	0 237 60017 X	Princess of Wales	0 237 60023 4
Mother Teresa	0 237 60008 0	Queen Victoria	0 237 60001 3
Margot Fonteyn	0 237 60033 1	Viv Richards	0 237 60027 7
Anne Frank	0 237 60015 3	Margaret Thatcher	0 237 60003 X
Elizabeth Fry	0 237 60028 5		
Gandhi	0 237 60011 0		
Indira Gandhi	0 237 60025 0		

Contents

Roald Dahl as many adults still think of him – the author of spooky short stories

1

Introduction

How would you describe your Grandma? Is she at all like George Kranky's? Bad luck if she is because nobody who met that particular lady could ever forget her:

'She was a selfish, grumpy old woman. She had pale brown teeth and a small puckered up mouth like a dog's bottom.'

In *George's Marvellous Medicine* George gets his own back on his dreadful relative — in a way, I hope, that could happen only in a story. But the chances are that you know already how he did it because the man who wrote the book is perhaps the most popular children's author who ever lived.

His name, and it was his real name, was Roald Dahl.

No other writer for children was as bold, as exciting, as rude or as funny as Roald Dahl. This is why creations like Grandma Kranky make many adults nervous. Probably most grown-ups should keep well away from Dahl's stories for children unless there's a youngster handy to help them cope with the shocking bits. For it's fair to say that the very best writing, whether for adults or children, always involves an element of *risk*. His success in taking this risk made Roald Dahl world-famous and a millionaire. He was, quite simply, a

From *George's Marvellous Medicine* (© Quentin Blake 1981)

superstar — someone who was often heard on the radio and seen on television, who was even recognized in the street (which is very unusual for a writer). Children were so keen to read his stories that in the year before he died in November 1991, his eighteen children's books in paperback sold more than two million copies in Britain alone.

What sort of person *was* Roald Dahl? Can we find out what he was really like?

Here we must face a problem that's best summed up by Dahl himself. 'There are two distinct sides to a writer of fiction,' he once said. 'First, there is the side he displays to the public, that of an ordinary person like anyone else, a person who does ordinary things and speaks an ordinary language. Second, there is the secret side which comes out in him only after he has closed the door of his work-room and is completely alone.'

Never forget as you read my account of Roald Dahl and his writing that his 'secret' side, which was by far the more important, can only be suggested or hinted at. Not even Dahl himself could explain fully how a story like *Charlie and the Chocolate Factory*, or a character like Fantastic Mr Fox, or even a gruesome piece of description like that of the Twit beard, was worked up into its final shape for the printed page. The way in which a writer 'grows' his books is as mysterious as the way in which The Big Friendly Giant mixes his dreams.

In comparison, dealing with the 'public' side of Roald Dahl is very straightforward since only someone as modest as he was could possibly call such a life *ordinary*. How ordinary is a life which contains the following?

... being shot down and crippled in an air-battle.
... becoming a spy.
... marrying a movie star.
... suffering the death of a daughter from a disease harmless to most children.

From *Fantastic Mr Fox* (© Jill Bennett 1974)

... inventing a special valve to help people who are
brain damaged.
... developing a revolutionary technique
for the after-care of stroke patients.
... learning to be an expert on paintings,
antique furniture, vintage wine
and the growing of orchids.

All this is in addition to the writing of scripts for the
cinema and television as well as novels and short stories
for adults — the last of which made Dahl's reputation
long before he turned to children's books.

To help me give the 'feel' as well as the facts about
this extraordinary man, I've called on Roald Dahl's
own words wherever I can, taking them from his books,
from articles about him, from conversations I had with
him. And I've assumed that you know already most of
his writing for young people.

If you don't, then read it first. You're in for a treat.

2

A Visit to Roald Dahl

Do you remember the scene in *Charlie and the Chocolate Factory* when Charlie Bucket finally gets lucky? Even then he almost misses his chance:

'I think,' he said quietly, 'I think . . . I'll have just one more of those chocolate bars. The same kind as before, please.'

'Why not?' the fat shopkeeper said, reaching behind him again and taking another Whipple-Scrumptious Fudgemallow Delight from the shelf. He laid it on the counter.

'Charlie picked it up and tore off the wrapper . . . and *suddenly* . . . from underneath the wrapper . . . there came a brilliant flash of gold.

'Charlie's heart stood still.

'It's a Golden Ticket!' screamed the shopkeeper, leaping about a foot in the air. 'You've got a Golden Ticket! You've found the last Golden Ticket! Hey, would you believe it! Come and look at this everybody! The kid's found Wonka's last Golden Ticket! There it is! It's right there in his hands!'

No wonder the shopkeeper is so excited and Charlie so stunned. The Golden Ticket is an invitation to tour

9

From *Charlie and the Chocolate Factory* (© George Allen & Unwin 1967)

the fabulous Chocolate Factory with its underground passageways and secret caverns where Willy Wonka and his assistants make their mouth-watering magic. Who wouldn't be thrilled to visit such a place?

Of course, the Wonka Factory doesn't exist in real life except in the pages of Roald Dahl's best-loved book. How and where was the tale itself invented, though? Was there a Roald Dahl Fiction Factory in which story-experiments were conducted over and over again till the right result came up — a Giant Peach or a Minpin or an Enormous Crocodile?

Is being a Writer much the same as being a Wonka?

The obvious way to find out would be to go and look — to fix up a meeting with the man behind the famous stories at the very place where he wrote them.

Sorry? That's impossible, you say, because Roald Dahl isn't alive any more?

You're right, of course ... except that *anything* is possible in a book. A book is like a Great Glass Elevator which can take you anywhere you like, travelling through time as well as space, because it's powered entirely by imagination.

Let's imagine then ...

You're standing in your local bookshop with a big smile on your face because you've just bought one of the last titles Roald Dahl wrote — *Esio Trot* (1990) perhaps, or *The Vicar Of Nibbleswicke* (1991). Suddenly as you flick through the pages, there's a brilliant flash of gold. It's a Golden Ticket just for you — your personal invitation to tour the best-known address in the world of children's books: Gipsy House, Great Missenden, Buckinghamshire, England.

Your heart stands still for a moment just like Charlie's.

Because now you've noticed the date on the ticket: Summer 1983. Yet the ticket is as fresh and brand new as the paperback you're holding in your hand! Does this mean Roald Dahl himself will be there? Will you be meeting him at about the time when *The BFG* (1982) had established him as the world's most popular living children's author?

In a trice, as easy as turning the page of a book, you find yourself in the High Street at Great Missenden late at night. You've got your overnight bag in your hand. Why does the place look so familiar? Then you

11

... a man you recognize at once

remember the first chapter of *The BFG*, when Sophie stares out of the orphanage window:

'In the silvery moonlight, the village street she knew so well seemed completely different. The houses looked bent and crooked, like houses in a fairy-tale. Everything was pale and ghostly and milky white.'

For a split second you're too scared to move. Where was it you were supposed to get directions? Ah, yes — The Red Lion Pub. A pub? At your age? Feeling as guilty as Danny The Champion of The World, when he took his first night drive, you enter the bar.

One glance at the Golden Ticket is enough for the man at the counter. He knows Roald Dahl — plays snooker with him at Gipsy House a couple of times a week. 'It's only five minutes walk even in the dark,' he says, and tells you how to get there.

Now you're at Gipsy House standing in a front porch that reminds you of a stone sentry-box.

Footsteps and loud barking answer your knock.

The door opens and you gape at a man you recognize at once.

'Hello,' he says. 'I'm Roald Dahl. Don't worry about the dogs. The black one's called Jelly and the honey-coloured one is Eva. They're very friendly — though Eva does sometimes nip people! Come on in — everyone's been looking forward to meeting you. We've got a nice lot of people staying for supper tonight.'

It's as if you've known him for years. In a way you have — from posters, magazines, books, radio and television. You remember reading somewhere that his long, friendly face with its crinkly, grey-blue eyes looks as though 'it had played the sheriff in a dozen Westerns'. He moves a bit like a sheriff, too, but that swaying walk doesn't come from wearing heavy sixguns at the hip: it's a leftover from several spine operations following the near fatal aircrash he described in *A Piece of Cake*, his first published story. But how, you wonder, did he ever get all two metres of him into the tiny cockpit of a fighter-plane? His chin must've been propped on his knees!

The other guests certainly *are* a nice lot of people.

13

A combination of sitting room, museum and art gallery

There's a woodcarver and her two daughters who are both art students, an American publisher over here to discuss the next Dahl tale, two Dutch girls who are currently managing the house, plus Lucy and Theo Dahl whose names are familiar to you from dedications in their father's books. No one gives you a chance to feel scared or left out. Best of all you like Theo, a warm and shy twenty-one-year old, still bubbling with excitement, as he tells you about Dahl and Son, the antique shop they've just opened in the High Street (you glanced in the window on your way to the house).

You feel very much at home ... except that this home is different from any other you've come across. Where else would you find such a combination of sitting-room, museum and art gallery? It's a lovely huddle of eye-catching paintings, old furniture and odd curios. As their owner answers questions about them you hear names great enough to make your art-teacher gasp — Matisse, Chippendale, Picasso, Henry Moore and the Russian painters Roald Dahl loves best of all: Malevich, Rodchenko, Goncharova, Popopa. Yet they're mention-ed so casually, even jokingly.

'See that little landscape behind you? I did it myself with housepaints then hung it there so I could pull the legs of the experts!'

'Aren't you proud of having such a collection?' someone asks.

'Not a bit. All it takes is a good eye — which helps you to buy them when they're cheap. Mind you, it does take money too. Before I was married I'd sell a story to the *New Yorker*, get $2,000 for it and go straight out and buy a picture, and then take a long time to write the next story and so have to sell the picture. Many paintings that today could be acquired only by millionaires decorated my walls for brief periods in the 1940s... in the end I finally managed to keep one or two and they built up.'

'Doesn't it cost a fortune in insurance?'

Dahl chuckles and shakes his head. 'Nothing at all. I refuse to insure them because that makes you think of the money side of it. To hell with that — if the house burns down, then that's just bad luck. I'd miss my pictures but money would be no compensation. It's the same with the furniture. I don't admire anyone who buys fine furniture: — or fine anything come to that — without troubling to study the history of the artists involved. You can't appreciate any work of art in the true sense until you've studied the personalities involved and the struggles they had.'

'Like Willy Wonka,' you blurt out.

The man who invented Willy Wonka roars with laughter.

'Exactly! Now there was a true artist.'

All through supper there's more laughing and teasing. Afterwards, as Roald Dahl shows you the rest of the house, you realize he's a person who refuses to be glum or stuck up even about matters he takes very seriously. His famous wine-cellar — 'bit of a glory-hole, this' — with its 4,000 bottles of vintage wine turns out to be functional rather than fancy. And when, from a bookcase at the foot of the stairs that's crammed with translations of his stories, he takes a version in Chinese he smiles in disbelief.

His own favourite room seems to be the one with the three-quarter size snooker table.

'Every Wednesday and Sunday at 6.30, The Boys come in to play,' he says with relish, 'and we don't stop for anything except hot sandwiches. There's Wally, the builder; Pete, who drives a van; Derek, who works for IPC; Tom, the plumber, who's scorer. Do you play?'

'Not yet,' you admit.

16

To tell the truth, your head's in a bit of a whirl. It's hard to get this gorgeous, cluttery, treasure-trove of a house straight in your mind. Where else could you come across a side-table on which stand several Edgar Allan Poe Awards for mystery writing alongside a genuine Oscar — awarded to Patricia Neal in 1964 for her part in the film *Hud*? Even the layout of the Dahl house is a splendid muddle: upstairs, the bedrooms of Roald, Theo, Tessa, Lucy and Ophelia seem to merge into each other with the occasional bathroom in between. You give up trying to work it out. All you need remember is that you're borrowing Sophie's room for the night — Tessa's daughter and Roald's grand-daughter. And the bathroom you'll be using is directly opposite; it's much scruffier than yours at home, you're glad to say, despite the carved Tudor doors on the wall cabinets. You must remember to tell Mum this.

But you can't get to sleep.

Even the cup of hot Bovril — Roald Dahl's favourite bed-time drink — doesn't help. Nor does the loan of his one surviving copy of *The Gremlins*, which is the first children's book he ever wrote almost fifty years ago. You must be one of the few children in the world who's read this yarn of the war-time Royal Air Force, with its bright Walt Disney style illustrations. This makes you feel very special ... but it also reminds you that you're no closer to solving the mystery. Nothing you've seen so far at Gipsy House corresponds to what Willy Wonka called 'the most important room in the entire factory ... all my most secret inventions are cooking and

17

Gipsy House

simmering in here'. He was referring to THE
INVENTING ROOM.

Where is Roald Dahl's INVENTING ROOM?
That's what you'd like to know most of all. It's true,
of course, that Willy Wonka kept his room locked up
and labelled PRIVATE — KEEP OUT but he still
allowed Charlie and Augustus and Veruca and Violet
and Mike to go inside and explore. Doesn't your Golden
Ticket give you the same privilege? You sigh, switch off
the light, and fall asleep.

After breakfast, Roald Dahl calls you outside. You have your first daytime view of Gipsy House. It's a white late-Georgian farmhouse with a slate roof, built around 1800. An extra annexe has been built on either side, though, and there are about two hectares of garden — carefully designed, he explains, 'to give maximum pleasure for minimum work'. Other buildings in the grounds reveal just how many-sided are your host's interests — a greenhouse, now empty but once containing prize-winning orchids; an aviary for housing parakeets; an indoor swimming pool.

'I can't offer you a swim, though, because the pool's drained out at present. It's full of old furniture I'm busy restoring for Theo's shop.'

'Is that where Danny and his Dad lived?' you ask, pointing to the trim, sky-blue gipsy caravan on the far side of the lawn.

'I suppose it was in a way. My sister and I bought it for an old roadmender friend of ours who had nowhere else to live. We moved it here when he died.'

'And what about that car?' you exclaim. 'It's a beauty!' Gleaming in the pale sunlight, the car fits almost exactly the description that opens one of your favourite Dahl short stories, *The Hitch Hiker*: 'I had a new car. It was an exciting toy, a big BMW 3.3 Li which means 3.3 litre, long wheel-base, fuel injection. It had a top speed of 129 mph and terrific acceleration ...'

'Ah, yes,' he murmurs, 'that's my real extravagance. Every year, if I can, I take a driving trip to France to visit friends.'

But you're not listening. You've stopped dead in your

19

The hut in which Roald Dahl wrote his books

tracks. A shed tucked behind the greenhouse has caught your eye — a plain, cobwebby shed that looks all the shabbier against the background of Buckinghamshire woods and fields. Why do you suddenly finger the Golden Ticket in your pocket?

'Is that . . .?'

'No one goes in there but me,' he says. 'The place hasn't been cleaned in years. Recently our nanny goat got in there and left droppings all over the floor. I thought, well that's going a bit far, so I swept them up.'

'So that's where . . .?'

'That's where I do the writing, yes. Would you like to see inside?'

'Please — I'd love to.'

THE INVENTING ROOM at last!

Nowhere could be less like the gigantic secret chamber of Willy Wonka. Here the walls are cracked and peeling, the floor a mess of litter, dust and old lino. A grimy plastic curtain droops over the window.

'Without that I'd end up watching the squirrels,' he explains. 'I'm in here between 10 and 12.30 every day, then break for lunch which is always the same: Norwegian prawns and half a lettuce. Afterwards I have a rest before coming back here from 4.00 till 6.00. It's heated by that ancient paraffin heater there, called an Aladdin. Also by this single-bar electric fire hanging from the ceiling which is directed at my hands.'

'May . . . may I see how you actually set about it — the writing, I mean?'

'Certainly.'

He steps into a sleeping-bag, pulls it up to his waist and settles himself in a faded wing-backed armchair. His feet he rests on a battered travelling case full of logs. This is roped to the legs of the armchair so its always at a perfect distance. He places a roll of corrugated paper across his knees and positions on top of this a flat, green board made from three-ply wood and shaped so it tucks under his elbows.

'Now I'm ready for work,' he says. 'Other things that are important are the six yellow pencils in this jar here — always six, there must be six. Also this automatic pencil-sharpener is vital and so is my red

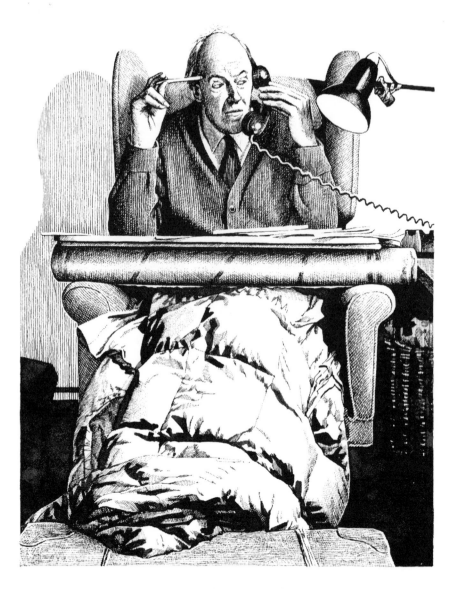

Roald Dahl at work

Thermos flask with coffee in it. I sip from it all the time.
I write on yellow paper, American legal it's called,
reading every sentence out loud to see if it *sounds* right

From *Charlie and the Chocolate Factory* (© George Allen & Unwin 1967)

and rubbing out what I don't like as I go along. This clothes-brush here is for getting rid of the shavings.'

'And that's it?' you ask.

'That's it.'

You gaze round in astonishment. Everything else in the hut — the grubby filing cabinets, the battered Anglepoise lamp, the huge wastepaper basket — might have come from a junk shop. Can this really be the workplace of the world's best-selling children's author? If you stumbled in on him by accident you'd think he was a tramp scribbling a begging letter.

'Not very pretty, is it,' Roald Dahl grins.

'No.'

'One of the nice things about being a writer is that all you need is what you've got in your head and a pencil and a bit of paper. You can do without special surroundings or expensive equipment.'

You stand there thinking how different this is from Charlie Bucket's first sight of Willie Wonka's vast chocolate factory. A question suddenly occurs to you.

'Is...is it possible then for *anyone* to become a writer?'

'Quite possible, yes.'

'Even me?'

His grin now seems to light up the hut as he sees that finally you've understood.

'Especially you,' he says.

It's the perfect end to your visit.

3

Before He Became a Writer

As you read about Roald Dahl's life, you'll notice he was an unusual man in at least two ways; firstly, he was a *gambler* — someone who not only lived dangerously for fun but who could grit his teeth and take a chance even when it was no fun at all; secondly, he was an *outsider* — a person who never quite behaved in the way people expected. These two aspects of his personality cropped up over and over again.

He was born in 1916 in Llandaff, Wales. Both his parents were Norwegian — his mother spoke English with a broad, heavy accent to the end of her life. She was his father's second wife, the first having died in childbirth. People died at what seems to us a very early age much more often in those days. Roald Dahl's father was one of them. Pneumonia killed him in 1919 only a month after the death of his own daughter, Dahl's sister, from appendicitis.

Harald Dahl was a clever, colourful character who'd lost an arm as a young man after he'd fallen from a roof. By the time he'd settled in Cardiff as a shipbroker he'd already run away twice to seek his fortune — from Norway and from France. In Wales he'd grown rich. Enough money was left in his will 'for good private

Roald and his mother at Cumberland Lodge

education and . . . good sized houses to live in with large gardens'. The Dahl house in Llandaff was called Cumberland Lodge right next door to Howell's school. Roald never forgot it.

'I used to climb on the high wall and look over at the girls. I was about eight or nine, I suppose.

'We had a lovely gardener, called Jones, who I was very friendly with, and my mother used to give us half-a-crown between us and we used to walk to the football ground, Ninian Park.

'Cardiff were in the First Division then. I'm talking about 1924 and we stood and watched these matches, the gardener and the little boy of eight. I loved it so much that I can still, nearly 70 years later, tell you the

On the beach at St Peter's

names of a number of the team.'

Till then, Roald Dahl had attended a local nursery (to which he rode every day by tricycle) followed by Llandaff Cathedral School. Now he was sent to a boarding prep school at Weston-Super-Mare called St Peter's. It changed his life. As soon as he got there he knew it was going to be 'the greatest torture in the world.'

For the full facts about St Peter's read 'Lucky Break' in *The Wonderful Story of Henry Sugar* which tells of the school's fierce discipline with its 'rules, rules and still more rules which had to be obeyed', of Mr Pople the paunchy, crimson-faced toady to the headmaster, and of the headmaster himself who would cane his pupils unmercifully 'for doing everything it was natural for small boys to do'.

This passage shows you what St Peter's boys had to put up with in those days — very different, I hope, from the school you attend:

'At the sound of the bell, all the boys in the school, one hundred and eighty of us, would move smartly to our positions in the corridor. We lined up against the walls on both sides and stood stiffly to attention, awaiting the headmaster's inspection.

'But at least ten minutes would elapse before the headmaster arrived on the scene, and during this time, Mr Pople would conduct a ceremony so extraordinary that to this day I find it hard to believe it ever took place. There were six lavatories in the school, numbered on their doors from one to six. Mr Pople, standing at the end of the long corridor, would have in the palm of his hand six small brass discs, each with a number on it, one to six. There was absolute silence as he allowed his eye to travel down the two lines of stiffly standing boys. Then he would bark out a name, 'Arkle!'

'Arkle would fall out and step briskly down the corridor to where Mr Pople stood. Mr Pople would hand him a brass disc. Arkle would then march away toward the entire length of the corridor, past all the stationary boys and then turn left. As soon as he was out of sight, he was allowed to look at his disc and see which lavatory number he had been given.

'Highton!' barked Mr Pople, and now Highton would fall out to receive his disc and march away.

'Angel!' ...
'Williamson!' ...
'Gaunt!' ...
'Price!' ...
'In this manner, six boys selected at Mr Pople's whim were dispatched to the lavatories to do their duty.'

Could it be that the rude and rollicking stories for children that Roald Dahl wrote many years later were a way of getting his own back on this poisonous place?

Yet, strangely enough, it was St Peter's which first set him on the path to becoming an author. This had nothing to do with the official curriculum, of course. If we're to believe one of his school reports, Dahl's writing and his boxing were on much the same level: 'too slow and ponderous. His punches are not well timed and are easily seen coming'. So much for the future short-story specialist! What saved St Peter's from being a complete disaster was a lady called Mrs O'Connor.

Every Saturday morning she'd arrive wearing a loose dress covered with amber beads and silver trinkets so she 'looked like a Christmas tree.' Her job was to be

'a sort of babysitter, to keep us quiet for two and a half hours while the masters went off boozing at the pub. But Mrs O'Connor was no babysitter. She was nothing less than a great and gifted teacher, a scholar and a lover of English Literature ... by the age of thirteen I had become intensely aware of the vast heritage of literature that had been built up in England over the centuries. I also became an avid and insatiable reader of good writing. Dear lovely Mrs O'Connor! Perhaps it was

Working for Shell in East Africa

worth going to that awful school simply to experience the joy of her Saturday mornings.'

Another joy for the young Roald was a very different kind of reading: comics. 'I *devoured* the *Beano* and the *Dandy* — couldn't get enough of them. I still have a letter I wrote home to mother which says 'by the way, where is my *Rainbow?*'

Roald Dahl chose his next school for himself: Repton. It was one of his unsuccessful gambles. The headmaster was the Reverend Geoffrey Fisher who later became Archbishop of Canterbury and crowned Queen Elizabeth II in Westminster Abbey — but he was no Mrs O'Connor. The beatings he handed out were the worst at the school, worse even than those of the prefects who at British Public Schools were allowed to cane younger pupils. Dahl hated all such legalized bullying, and many years afterwards wrote a short story for adults about it (called 'Galloping Foxley' in *Someone Like You*) as well as a spine-chilling account for children in Chapter 12 of *Danny Champion of the World*. At the time, according to the school, he could still barely string a half-dozen words together. His report for the Summer Term 1930 was typical: 'I have never met a boy who so persistently writes the exact opposite of what he means. He seems incapable of marshalling his thoughts on paper'.

What he *was* good at was sport and exams. While at Repton he was heavyweight boxing champion, captain of fives, played for the football and squash teams and became a scratch-golfer. Also he amazed his house-master by passing his school certificate (similar to today's GCSE) with a Credit in all eight subjects. Not a bad record, you may think, for someone who never became a prefect himself because 'the general feeling was that I was not reliable and didn't take anything seriously'. Certainly it's hard to imagine the future creator of Mr and Mrs Twit fitting easily into the sort of school which requires its pupils to wear a black tail-coat, a black tie worn with a stiff, butterfly collar, striped trousers and a straw hat.

But where *would* the young Dahl fit in? Not Oxford or Cambridge, he decided. He'd had quite enough of formal education. All he really wanted to do was travel. This longing was confirmed when he went on a trip to Newfoundland with the British Public Schools Exploring Expedition. He was the group's official photographer; and its unofficial rebel since, always the odd man out, he led a mutiny against the expedition

Roald as a trainee pilot in Nairobi

leader, Commander Murray Levick, who had been in the Antarctic with Captain Scott.

After this he joined the Shell Oil Company. When his training was finished he was summoned to Head Office. Would he please pack his bags and accept a three-year posting to Egypt? No, said Dahl. Why not? Because 'it's too dusty there'. Shell were so astonished at his cheek that they agreed to send him where he'd always wanted to go: East Africa.

His two years in Tanganyika (now Tanzania) felt like a reward for the miseries he'd suffered at school: 'It was a fantastic life. The heat was intense but who cared? Our dress was khaki shorts, an open shirt and topee on the head. I learned to speak Swahili. I drove up country visiting diamond mines, sisal plantations, gold mines and all the rest of it. There were giraffes, elephants, zebras, lions and antelopes all over the place'.

Not that the living was easy since this Paradise also

included snakes, scorpions and mosquitoes. Like everyone else he got malaria and lay for three days with a temperature of one hundred and five point five. But it was all a great adventure — 'fantastically exciting'. What brought it to a close was an even greater, tougher and more tragic adventure. In September 1939 Britain declared war on Hitler's Germany.

Roald Dahl's first experience of action wasn't against the enemy but against his friends. As a Special Reservist, he was ordered to stop Tanganyika's German residents from escaping. Many of them he knew personally. When they reached the road-block he'd set up, he ordered them to stop ... or be machine-gunned. Luck was with him this time and 'in the cool of the evening, we marched them all back to Dar-es-Salaam where they were put into a huge camp surrounded by barbed wire'.

After this he decided to join the RAF — mainly because the Navy was too far away and being a soldier, he suspected, would involve more marching. So he drove to Nairobi and volunteered. Six months' training followed — skimming all over Kenya in a Tiger Moth so small his legs were crunched up almost under his chin and his head jutted far out of the cockpit. He finished his training in Iraq, passing out as an officer top of his class. Of the twenty pilots in his group, seventeen were later killed during the war.

While training, pilots were never sure whether they'd be assigned to bombers, which called for team-membership, or fighters, which suited individualists. Perhaps you can guess the RAF's decision about Roald Dahl: he was sent to 80 Squadron which flew fighters. At first he was based in the Western Desert of Libya flying against the Italians in an ancient single-seater bi-plane called a Gloster Gladiator. This had two machine-guns mounted on either side of the engine which fired their bullets by a carefully synchronized process *through* the propellor blades ... most of the time, that is. It was not unknown for a Gladiator pilot to shoot himself down instead of his opponent. The plane had other disadvantages, too, not least that it caught fire very easily — as Dahl discovered when he crashlanded between enemy lines. He managed to crawl from his wrecked aircraft before it exploded but he was burned, blinded and his nose was smashed into his face. And these were just the injuries that were put right after six months in an Alexandria hospital. For the rest of his life Roald suffered from the damage the crash did to his spine. Both of his hips were eventually removed and replaced by false, steel equivalents — he used one of the

34

originals (called the femur) as a paperweight!

Many years later in his autobiographical books *Boy* (1984) and *Going Solo* (1986) which topped the best-seller lists for both children's and adult's books, Roald Dahl gave his own account of the events in this early life that I've summarized here. Nowhere, though does he describe his plane-crash better than he does in the story 'A Piece of Cake' which he wrote in 1942.

As with most writers at the start of their careers, Roald Dahl's early 'fiction' sticks very closely to the fact of his own experience:

'There was nothing to worry about. Nothing at all. Not until I felt the hotness around my legs. At first it was only a warmness and that was all right too, but all at once it was a hotness, a very stinging scorching hotness up and down the sides of each leg ... I turned the buckle, released the parachute harness and with some effort hoisted myself up and tumbled over the side of the cockpit. Something seemed to be burning so I rolled about a bit in the sand, then crawled away from the fire on all fours and lay down.

'I heard some of my machine-gun ammunition going off in the heat and I heard some of the bullets thumping into the sand nearby. I did not worry about them; I merely heard them.

'Things were beginning to hurt. My face hurt most. There was something wrong with my face. Something had happened to it. Slowly I put a hand to feel it. It was sticky. My nose didn't seem to be there. I tried to feel my teeth, but I cannot remember whether I came to any conclusion about them. I think I dozed off.'

It was the headaches that worried him most, though. He re-joined his squadron, now flying Hurricanes, and saw more action in Greece, Crete, Palestine and the Lebanon. But by the summer of 1941, with a personal tally of five enemy aircraft shot down, his career as a pilot was over. He was invalided back to England and given a month's leave. By now his mother, brother and four sisters had moved to Buckinghamshire, having been bombed out of the family house in Kent during the Battle of Britain. When he arrived unexpectedly at their small, thatched cottage, he had a kitbag stuffed full with limes and oranges — a coming-home present after four years away.

Not that he stayed in England long. By January 1942 he had a new assignment. Once again it had come about quite by chance — a meeting with Sir Harold Balfour, the number two man in the Air Ministry, at Pratts Club in London. Flight Lieutenant Roald Dahl, it seemed, was just the man to go to the United States of America as Assistant Air Attaché.

As what? Three days after he'd arrived he was still wondering what he was supposed to be doing. Then came a knock at the door of his Washington DC office. In walked a small, shy man who wore thick steel-rimmed spectacles. Would the new Attaché have lunch with him and tell him all about being a fighter pilot? You see, he was hoping to write a series of articles for *The Saturday Evening Post*. His name was C.S. Forester. No, he wasn't joking. He really *was* C.S. Forester!

To Roald Dahl's astonishment he was soon in a

restaurant talking to one of the most famous authors alive, whose sea stories — especially about Captain Horatio Hornblower — were popular the world over. Or rather, he wasn't talking. 'Somehow the roast duck, vegetables, potatoes and thick rich gravy kept getting in the way.' At this point Roald Dahl took another chance. Would Mr Forester prefer a written account instead which he could re-write in his own time?

That night Roald Dahl put together his first ever story. The next day a secretary in the Embassy typed it out and sent it off. And two weeks later this letter arrived, a report on Roald Dahl's use of language which would have astonished his teachers:

'Dear RD, You were meant to give me notes, not a finished story. I'm bowled over. Your piece is marvellous. It is the work of a gifted writer. I didn't touch a word of it. I sent it at once under your name to my agent, Harold Matson, asking him to offer it to the *Saturday Evening Post* with my personal recommendation. You will be happy to hear that the *Post* accepted it immediately and have paid one thousand dollars. Mr Matson's commission is ten per cent. I enclose his check for nine hundred dollars. It's all yours. As you will see from Mr Matson's letter, which I also enclose, the *Post* is asking if you will write more stories for them. I do hope you will. Did you know you were a writer? With my very best wishes and congratulations, C.S. Forester.'

No, Roald Dahl hadn't known before that he was a writer. But he knew now.

4

After He Became a Writer

Someone once asked the great English comic novelist, P.G. Wodehouse, what the secret was to being an author. He's said to have replied, 'You keep your bum on a chair'. This is the after-the-workroom-door-is-closed side of writing which I mentioned in the first chapter. There are very few authors whose life is as fascinating as their books. It's important that you keep this in mind because Roald Dahl was one of the exceptions. Even after he'd settled down to being a family man, so many dramatic and unexpected events actually happened to him that it's easy in his case to overlook the odd, lonely existence going on at the same time which no author can avoid.

At first, being posted to the United States seemed to bring him nothing but good luck. His job at the Embassy put him in touch with the most important people in America. So did his writing. After the publication of his first book for children — *The Gremlins* — he was given three weeks leave to go to Hollywood where Walt Disney wanted to turn it into a film:

'I was put up at Disney's expense in the luxurious Beverley Hills Hotel and given a huge shiny car to drive

Roald Dahl and Walt Disney

about in. Each day I worked with the great Disney at his studios in Burbank ... I mooched around the rooms where the gifted and obstreperous animators worked, the men who had already created *Snow White*, *Dumbo*, *Bambi* and other marvellous films.'

Alas, *The Gremlins* as a movie was never finished but the book attracted much attention. Soon every airman in the world knew the name of these little creatures who lived in RAF fighter-planes and bombers — and who caused the damage, the breakdowns and the crashes for which the enemy always got the blame. Even the President of the United States heard about them and invited Roald Dahl to the White House:

'In there, believe it or not, I spent a great deal of time

with Franklin Roosevelt during his relaxing hours . . . and he would say things like, 'I've just had an interesting cable from Mr Churchill'. Then he would tell me what it said, something perhaps about new plans for the bombing of Germany or the sinking of U-boats, and I would do my best to appear calm and chatty, though actually I was trembling at the realization that the most powerful man in the world was telling me these mighty secrets.'

This sort of information was crucial for Roald Dahl's job. By now he'd discovered exactly what an Assistant Air Attaché was supposed to do. He was mainly a gatherer of Intelligence — which is a polite way of describing a spy. At this time, remember, the United States hadn't yet entered the fighting and it was vital that Britain knew America's intentions. So when Dahl was shown a document from Vice President Henry Wallace that outlined America's plans to take over Europe's commercial airlines after the war, he took one of his gambles and borrowed it for a while. It was. initiative like this which eventually got him summoned back to England to meet 'the fabulous 'C', the head of the Secret Service. 'C' was anxious to know everything that was going on in America. When Roald Dahl returned to Washington he'd been promoted to the rank of Wing Commander. This was just as well because the other side of his nature had also cropped up once again: he'd been sacked from his Embassy post because he 'just didn't fit in'.

After the war he decided to settle in Amersham,

Buckinghamshire. His work still took him regularly across the Atlantic, though — at first when he was commissioned to write the official history of the Strategic Intelligence Service and later because it was American journals which paid him best for his stories: *The New Yorker, Collier's, Harper's Magazine, Cosmopolitan* and *The Saturday Evening Post*. Nowadays it's difficult to believe that a writer could live comfortably if he sold only two short stories a year to such publications, but for almost twenty years this is just what Roald Dahl did.

It meant much closing of that workroom door, of course. Sometimes he'd slave for a month on the first page of a new story. His early tales, mostly about flyers and flying, were reprinted in a book called *Over to You*. No one took much notice of it, perhaps because his writing-style at this time was too close to that of Ernest Hemingway, the famous novelist who later became a great friend.

There's nothing strange about this — most writers need time to find a personal 'voice'. Their early work is often written under the influence of an admired model.

Dahl's next book was an anti-war fantasy with the title *Sometime Never*, but again it attracted little attention. What brought success, and made him world-famous, was the gathering together of his funny, spooky magazine stories in two collections called *Someone Like You* and *Kiss Kiss*. These have a flavour that's instantly recognizable. They're written in a sharp, clear style that almost anyone can cope with, but their subject matter makes them more suitable for

Patricia Neal

adults than children. So postpone reading them till you are older if you want full enjoyment. For a preview of the quirkiness and unexpected endings that have become almost a Dahl trademark, re-read two stories from *Henry Sugar*: 'The Boy Who Talked With Animals' and 'The Hitch-hiker'.

By now Roald Dahl was equally at home in Amersham and in New York where his friends included writers like Lillian Hellman and John O'Hara, musicians like Leonard Bernstein ... or actresses like Patricia Neal. He met her on 20 October 1952 at 6.45 pm — the page from his pocket diary, mounted in a small frame, stood for years on a side table in the Dahl living room. The following year Patricia Neal and Roald Dahl were married. Soon afterwards he had a letter from England to say that a small Georgian farmhouse with two hectares was up for sale in Great

Missenden: Gipsy House. It was bought in an auction at the village pub for £4,250.

It's hard now to get a clear picture of this famous pair — the Oscar-winning film-star and the best-selling author — because so much ballyhoo surrounds what happened to them. Probably, even without what Roald Dahl calls 'the disasters', the marriage would have been no ordinary one. Pat was the 'most independent woman I ever knew' and Roald, if anyone, deserved the word he used in *Danny The Champion of the World* to describe Danny's Dad ... 'sparky'. So the next few years were bound to be eventful as they shifted between Hollywood and Great Missenden each committed to different careers and very different lives, but each also intent on the family they both so much wanted. At about two-to-three year intervals, Olivia, Tessa, Theo, Ophelia and Lucy were born. A similar interval separates each of the three famous disasters which occurred between 1960 and 1965.

First came Theo's. He was only four months old when a taxi hit his pram at the corner of 82nd Street and Madison Avenue in New York, slamming him into a passing bus. He was battered about the head, temporarily blinded, and even after a series of operations was left with the condition known as hydrocephalus or water-on-the-brain. This led his father with the help of a neuro-surgeon at Great Ormond Street Children's Hospital, London and an aeroplane modeller living near Great Missenden to invent the DWT valve (Dahl-Wade-Till), a non-blocking gadget implanted in the brain to drain away excess fluid. Such resourcefulness was matched only by Dahl's courage when Theo, at the age of four, needed to have this shunt-valve taken out if he was to move on to the next stage of his recovery. The doctors dithered, knowing the risks. Roald Dahl, also knowing the risks, relied on his gambler's instinct. He and Pat took turns to watch Theo day and night after the valve was removed. Theo got better and better. On the kitchen wall at Gipsy House was hung the prototype of Theo's valve, a memento of bad luck turned to good account.

Another, and sadder, memento to misfortune is the dedication of *The BFG*. This reads: 'For Olivia ... 20 April 1955 — 18 November 1962'. She died from a rare complication of measles even though one of the country's leading doctors had been consulted, who assured the family that there was nothing at all to cause concern. The shock and upset drove the Dahls to talk to Geoffrey Fisher, who by now was head of the Church of England. Would he turn out to be a better Archbishop than he'd been a headmaster? Not much, according to Dahl.

Nor was this the end of the family troubles. In 1965 the Dahls were in Hollywood again. Roald was writing, Patricia was just starting a film for MGM called *Seven Women*. She was also pregnant with her fifth baby. Then, at six o'clock one evening, she had a rupture of the brain called an aneurism. Massive internal bleeding followed. She was rushed to the University College of Los Angeles Medical Centre where a seven-hour emergency operation was performed. At the end the surgeon said 'she'll live', but added, 'I don't know if I've

From *Matilda* (© Quentin Blake, 1988, Jonathan Cape)

done her a favour'. She was brought back to Gipsy House with double vision, a near-useless arm and leg on her right side and unable to cope with simple activities like reading, counting, talking or remembering the names of her own children.

Even people who've never read a word of Roald Dahl, or seen a clip from a Patricia Neal movie know the story of what came next. It's been publicized in countless newspapers and magazines, broadcast on radio and television, summarized in a book by Barry Farrell called *Pat and Roald* and turned into a screen version that starred Glenda Jackson and Dirk Bogarde with the title *The Patricia Neal Story*. One of the main attractions of this tall but true tale is that Patricia and Roald survived this disaster. Yet success didn't come easily.

Two factors brought it about: first, sheer guts on her part; second, a coming together of his ability to take risks and his 'outsider' instinct for when expert opinion isn't to be trusted. Straightaway he rejected the local hospital's proposal of two visits a week by a speech therapist: 'That would have been useless. She had the mentality of a four year-old. I could see nothing very special about this speech therapy — I thought the thing that was needed was stimulation. You must combat the enormous depression and the bit where they get suicidal.' So he organized a roster of friends to give almost round-the-clock attention: talk, lessons, puzzles, games — anything that would warm up a seemingly deep-frozen brain. It was relentless, ruthless and for some people very, very wrong. He admitted, 'I was often heavily criticized for pushing her too hard'.

But it worked. In August 1965 Lucy was born without difficulty. A year later Patricia Neal could walk and talk again. In 1967 she started shooting a new film, *The Subject Was Roses*.

If real life were like a cinema film or a fairy story the Dahls would have lived happily ever after following such a triumph. Alas, though, their lives were moving apart. Had the 'disasters' taken their toll at last? Did the contradiction in life-style between an actress and writer, each with an outsize personality, finally wear their relationship out? Probably it was something of both, though no one can be sure — not even the couple themselves. In 1983, when the stress of their situation was no longer bearable, Patricia Neal and Roald Dahl were divorced. Later that year Roald married Felicity

Pat and Roald

D'Abreu, known as Liccy, a family friend who was his partner for the rest of his life.

The courage and determination Pat and Roald had shown when the future seemed blackest had a marvellous outcome, though.

Valerie Eaton Griffith, one of the people who'd helped them, developed this new technique of therapy into an organization called The Volunteer Stroke Scheme which is now allied to the Chest and Heart Association. Today there are more than forty branches throughout Britain and Northern Ireland each with about 100 members. Such success gave Roald Dahl special satisfaction because 'I've always loved the medical sciences. If my father had lived I'd have studied and become a doctor.'

Instead he was a writer. This is a notoriously unreliable way to earn money — especially if you're distracted with family problems, almost bankrupted by medical bills and the studio has cut off your wife's salary, as MGM did Pat's. Film-scripts were one source of income, notably for the James Bond movie *You Only Live Twice* (1967) and, though his words were never in fact used, for *Chitty-Chitty Bang-Bang* (1968). Except for the Bond film which he enjoyed immensely, Roald Dahl preferred to forget his script-writing efforts. Years later he declared, 'Nobody writes screenplays except for money. You don't do it otherwise. I don't need money now, so I don't do them'.

What made his fortune was a shift in the direction of his writing. For this, thanks must go to Olivia, Tessa, Theo, Ophelia and Lucy.

'I used to tell them a different made-up story every night. Some of them were pretty rotten but with one or two a child would say, 'Can we have more of what you told us last night?' And so I started to write *James and the Giant Peach*. I liked doing it so much I went straight on to *Charlie*.'

It was *Charlie and the Chocolate Factory*, published in 1964, which established Roald Dahl as the superstar of children's storytellers. Not that it was an overnight success. In its first year it sold 5,000 hardback copies in America ... then 6,000, 18,000, 35,000, 85,000 and 125,000 for each of the following five years. Now three decades after it first appeared, it still sells in paperback at the rate of more than 100,000 copies annually. According to the British paperback company Puffin, other Dahl titles have a similar standing as 'permanent children's classics'. As a children's author Roald Dahl was, and still is, at 'the very top of the league' and there's what Puffin call 'a quantum difference' between him and his closest rivals. Even a book of verse was a bestseller when Roald Dahl wrote it — as witness the 60,000 hardback copies of *Revolting Rhymes* sold in 1982. Children are familiar with all the tales in it — but not the way they're told here. See, for instance, the ending of 'Little Red Riding Hood and the Wolf':

'That's wrong!' cried Wolf. 'Have you forgot
to tell me what BIG TEETH I've got?
Ah well, no matter what you say,
I'm going to eat you anyway."
The small girl smiles. One eyelid flickers.
She whips a pistol from her knickers.
She aims it at the creature's head
And *bang, bang, bang,* she shoots him dead.
A few weeks later, in the wood,
I came across Miss Riding Hood.
But what a change! No cloak of red,
No silly hood upon her head,
She said, "Hello, and do please note
My lovely furry WOLFSKIN COAT.'

Over the years Roald Dahl undertook other writerly enterprises, of course. A third collection of tales, *Switch Bitch*, was published in 1965 and in 1979 came a second novel for adults, *My Uncle Oswald*. Also many of his short stories were adapted and televised world-wide in the series *Tales of the Unexpected*. Another book of verse called *Dirty Beasts* was issued in 1983 and in the autumn came *The Witches* which he claimed 'examines the world of witches in the same way as *The BFG* examined the world of giants'.

In many ways *The Witches* is a typical Dahl book — a mixture of quirky plot, a surprise finish and a hefty dose of cheekiness on every page. Few readers will miss the hickory-dickory-dock joke towards the end, for example, or the trick Dahl plays at the beginning when he suggests that the teacher who's reading the story aloud to her class might *herself* be a witch! In one respect, though, the book marked a turning point for Roald Dahl: for the first time ever he won a literary-prize awarded by *adults*. *The Witches* came first in the children's section of the prestigious Whitbread Award ... and Dahl's own response was typical. Straightaway, he gave his £3,000 prize-money to Helen House Hospice, in Oxford — the only hospital in the country for children so ill they're not expected to recover. 'I was pleased and honoured to get the Whitbread,' he remarked, 'but the Children's Book Award, which was a lovely little pamphlet, meant a lot more because it was chosen by the kids . . .'. This, for *The BFG*, had been awarded the previous year, a prize Dahl won again with *Matilda* in 1989.

By the second half of the nineteen-eighties, in fact, his success as a writer for young people was acknowledged by almost everyone — which didn't mean, of course, that everyone was pleased about it. Right to the end of his life Roald Dahl retained that streak of the outsider and gambler who could be relied upon to speak his mind regardless of the opinions other people might have preferred him to have. He never lost his relish for teasing, or for pricking the pretensions of anyone he regarded as pompous or stuck-up. It's no accident that so many of his stories describe the downfall of someone in authority — such as the awful headteacher Miss Trunchbull in *Matilda* (1988).

Children, of course, love the sheer dottiness of such characters however far removed they are from everyday reality. Year by year, the sales-figures for Roald Dahl's books grew — along with the mail he received from youngsters all over the world and the demands on his time and attention that soon came with international celebrity status. Did you know, for instance, that Roald Dahl was a member of the panel that in 1989 helped set up the English part of Britain's National Curriculum for schools?

Not for long, though. 'Too boring,' he declared and quickly resigned.

Where he was happiest, after all, was in that ramshackle hut in his orchard. There, in his battered armchair with his sleeping bag tucked around his legs and a pad and pencil to hand, he could travel anywhere he fancied and do anything he chose with no restrictions at all. On the last page of *The Minpins* (1991) Roald Dahl advises his readers to 'watch with glittering eyes the whole world around you because the greatest secrets are always hidden in the most unlikely places. Those who don't believe in magic will never find it'. And the best place to find magic, he seems to be reminding us, is in our own imagination.

51

5

Roald Dahl and the Movies

Imagine that you've been asked to write a film-script. You've been told not to worry about the cost or about any technical difficulties — these will be dealt with by someone else. Your job is to think up the most thrilling scenes you can for a spy movie that's meant to be funny as well as exciting.

This, broadly, was what Roald Dahl set out to do when he took on the screenplay for the fifth James Bond film, *You Only Live Twice*. What did he come up with? Here are just four of his ideas:

— a hi-jacking in outer space with one spacecraft swallowing up another.

— a fake sea-burial in which the 'corpse' is later rescued by frogmen.

— an air battle between miniature helicopters above the crater of a volcano.

— a motorway chase during which the villains' car is snatched up by a giant magnet and dumped in the sea.

Does all this sound exciting? Well, so it was. The man who wrote all the Bond novels, Ian Fleming, had been a great friend of Roald Dahl, and his famous central character — Commander James Bond (007) — was a

52

A famous scene from the film *You Only Live Twice*

larger-than-life hero Roald very much enjoyed. As an ex-spy himself, Roald was unlikely to take Bond's exploits too seriously. At the same time he admired the character's flair, self-reliance, gambling instinct and sheer zest for life. Altogether, he seemed the perfect choice for the project. He looked back on it as being one of the happiest periods of his working life. Alas, though, the movie turned out for Roald to be a case of you only live *once*. All his other involvements in the

world of film-making were a disaster. It's a world which
tends to be very tough indeed for a writer.

Why?

In this chapter we take a look at the sort of problems
an author faces when he writes for the cinema. The
rewards, of course, are very high. But once a writer steps
out of his study and on to the film-set he's surrendered
control over his material in two important ways.

The first of these is easy to understand. In his own
workroom an author is a solo performer. Words are the
start and finish of his business and finding the right
ones is his main concern. On the floor of a film studio,
though, he must take his place amongst a whole team of
performers — actors and actresses, experts in stunts and
special effects, designers and make-up artists, costume
and continuity advisers, camera-men and lighting
crew. These are just some of the scores of people who
have a contribution to make. A studio is more like a
circus than a study.

Secondly, the writer isn't even the ringmaster of the
show. At least two other people could equally claim to
be the 'author' of the film being made: the producer,
who organizes the project and who usually stands to
lose most if it goes wrong; and the director, who's in
charge of shooting. Both these people have far more
power than the writer to decide what ends up on the
cinema-screen.

This doesn't mean that the writer has no importance.
Often he's paid a great deal of money for the right to
film his book — and even more if he agrees to provide
his own screenplay. But what he does give up is the final

say in what happens to it. A good example of why this can be crucial is the film of *Charlie and the Chocolate Factory*. When filming began in 1971 it was already well on the way to becoming one of the most popular children's books ever written. Roald Dahl himself agreed to write the script. So wasn't it certain to be a huge success? Far from it! The critic Leslie Halliwell was surely being kind to the film when he said that it . . . 'Looks good but never seems quite happy with itself'. What had gone wrong?

Just about everything, according to Roald Dahl. It was the biggest disappointment of his career. Almost at once he realized how much was to be altered — including the plot, the central character and the whole atmosphere of the original story. 'I remember the director saying, 'Of course, you know this little boy Charlie is a wet — he's no good at all. We've got to jazz him up.' I gaped at him but I wasn't senior enough at the time to say 'go to hell', which I should've done. Later I would. I'd have walked out. But like an idiot — I really take the blame — I went along with it because we needed the money then. We had all sorts of expenses.' So, unhappily, he re-wrote a script that grew further and further away from the book on which it was based. Even the title was changed to *Willy Wonka and the Chocolate Factory*. The reason for this was typical of the shift in approach. 'They wanted a Hollywood star to play Willy Wonka and I wanted a wild and zany Englishman — Spike Milligan or Peter Sellers.' For a while, Roald thought he'd won this battle at least. Spike Milligan was so keen to play the part he even shaved off his beard to show the director what he looked like without it. But in the end it was the American actor Gene Wilder who was chosen. 'He was completely and utterly wrong. He played it for subtle, adult laughs and all the funny jokes I'd managed to write in he threw away. You've got to play it broad ... it's exactly like a pantomime. If we'd had Milligan or Sellers romping through it and a hundred children playing the Oompa-Loompas, we'd have had a fantasy like *The Wizard of Oz*. But they ruined it.' Next time you see the movie make sure you re-read the book, too, and ask yourself which version you prefer. Do you share Roald Dahl's doubts about the film? Or was he too hard on Hollywood?

To see a good book spoiled is probably the worst thing that can happen to a writer in the film industry. Almost as bad, though, is to see your work not reaching the screen at all. This happened three times to Roald Dahl. *The Gremlins* and *Chitty-Chitty-Bang-Bang* were mentioned in earlier chapters. More frustrating still was the tale of the first film-script he ever wrote, called *Sting-a-Ling*. He'd based this on an idea by Robert Altman, who at the time was a little-known television director. If Hollywood liked the script, Dahl promised, Altman would direct the movie. To his delight he was offered a price of $150,000. 'Okay,' I said, 'but Mr Robert Altman must direct it.' 'Robert Altman!' they cried. 'Are you crazy? He's a television director.' In the end the project went ahead only after Dahl had given Altman half his fee as compensation ... but not very far ahead. The director who was appointed instead of Altman abandoned the film after only a month. This was especially infuriating because Robert Altman went on to become one of America's top directors. 'They couldn't recognize talent when they saw it staring them in the face,' Dahl commented.

Perhaps now you can understand why writing screenplays can be highly profitable but very unsatisfactory. What isn't so clear yet is the sheer thrill of working on a film when things go right. Roald Dahl's experience with *You Only Live Twice* (1967) illustrates this. The project began for him with an unexpected phone-call to Gipsy House, offering him the job. Soon afterwards a film-projector was sent to him along with an operator and each of the first four Bond movies that had been made. Over and over again Roald watched them to familiarize himself with the pattern they always followed. Apart from this he was given a free hand. And here he had a stroke of luck. The director of the film was to be Lewis Gilbert — not only very experienced but a man who trusted a good writer. 'Go ahead and write it,' Gilbert said when they first met. 'Make it up. Go where you want.' A second stroke of luck was Ian Fleming's novel — which is one of the weakest of his books. So little turned out to be worth keeping that there was no original to spoil. Apart from the title the rest was up to Dahl. He seized the opportunity. Here's the opening scene:

'1. LONG SHOT — THE UNIVERSE

The camera moves past planets and stars and ends on a CLOSE SHOT OF THE WORLD. Suddenly into the

57

foreground a spacecraft fills the screen. Painted large on its body is the UNITED STATES FLAG and the words UNITED STATES.'

530 scenes later we reach the closing scene:

'531. EXT. SEA — DINGHY AND SUBMARINE — DAWN

Higher and higher rises the dinghy, perched upon the corner tower of M's submarine. Submarine surfaces and we

FADE OUT

In between, James Bond saves the earth from his sinister enemy Blofeld who is trying to provoke World War III so he can be boss of whatever's left when it's over. The script moves at a madcap pace, refuses to take itself seriously and makes full use of a range of gadgets so spectacular they might have come from a spy-factory run by Willy Wonka.

A great deal of effort went into it, of course. Roald had to meet a tight deadline and was often hard at work by five o'clock in the morning. Writing for the screen is not at all like the sort of storytelling that's intended to be read or heard. Different talents are called for —mostly an eye for action, an ear for dialogue and the ability to get the balance right between the two. Take, for instance, the chase sequence. What makes this so memorable is the way it ends: a huge magnet suspended from a helicopter, has sucked up the gangsters' car to stop them machine-gunning James Bond and his girlfriend Saki. The screen-writer mustn't tell this though. He must let the camera 'show' it. Page 51 of the

156C. EXT. SKY WITH TOKYO IN B.G. - SIKORSKY   156C.
       HELICOPTER, BLACK SEDAN - DAY

High up now, the Helicopter is carrying the Sedan away.
CAMERA shooting TOWARDS Tokyo to give impression Helicopter
is over the city.

156D. INT. BLACK SEDAN - AIRBORNE - DAY   156D.

DRIVER.   TWO GUNMEN.
The terrified occupants are being thrown about a good deal
as Black Sedan sways on end of cable.

156E. EXT. SKY AND SEACOAST - SIKORSKY HELICOPTER   156E.
       AND BLACK SEDAN - DAY

Helicopter is over the ocean, coast in b.g. Sedan is still
dangling below. Helicopter drops Sedan into the water.

(NOTE: This scene may be more effective if placed at the
        end of Scene 157.)

157. INT. SPORTS CAR - FREEWAY - DAY   157.

BOND.   SUKI.
SUKI flicks switch under dash. TANAKA again appears in
colour on T.V. SCREEN.

                    SUKI
                 (into speak-box)
              Thank you.

                    TANAKA
                 (on T.V.)
              Zero, zero...

                    BOND
                 (into speak-box)
              Yes.

                    TANAKA
                 (on T.V.)
              Motor Vessel Ningpo is owned by
              Osato Chemicals, Tokyo.....

Page 51 of Roald Dahl's script for *You Only Live Twice*.
Script copyright © 1966 Danjag S.A.

script demonstrates how he does this. The following
points are worth noting:

1. The writing is as much for the people behind the
   camera as in front of it.

2. Scene 156 is broken down into different camera-shots, but the director is left to decide on their final order.
3. There's very little dialogue — only fifteen or so words between six performers who are given no 'acting' instructions. These, too, are left to the director.
4. The 'feel' here is very much of work-in-progress rather than a piece that's fixed and finished.

The last point is especially important. Flexibility is essential on a film-set. Hold-ups can occur at any time — such as the special permission that producers had to get before they were allowed to drop the car in Tokyo Bay. Yes, this does mean it actually happened! All the stunts in the film were genuine. Notice, too, the phrase at the top of the page, 'Revised 21st August'. By this stage Roald Dahl had joined the film company in Japan where the film was being shot. 'I can remember sitting in the middle of shooting which cost something like twenty thousand dollars a day and if Lewis Gilbert needed a new scene I'd write it. I'd say, 'Here's another ten pages for you,' and we'd meet in the coffee-shop at the Tokyo Hilton and he'd just glance through them and say 'That's super. We'll shoot it tomorrow.'

And shoot it they did — almost exactly as scripted. It was a perfect partnership. 'The whole thing was a pleasure,' Roald Dahl said afterwards, 'because the director respected the writer and vice-versa. You all kept in your own provinces ... you did the things you were good at. That's why it was fun and that's why it came off.' About this film, Leslie Halliwell wrote, 'The Bond saga at its most expensive and most expansive. Full of local colour and in-jokes with an enormously impressive set for the climatic action.'

If all Roald Dahl's experience with film-making had been like *You Only Live Twice* there might have been many more Dahl movies. But it was his only screen success — including, to his dismay, the films that were made of his most popular stories. He was so upset by *Willy Wonka and the Chocolate Factory* that he refused all film-offers for years till, following in swift succession came *Danny Champion of the World* (1989), *The BFG* (1990), and *The Witches* (1990). You must make your own mind up how enjoyable they are. Dahl had his own opinion. He thought all three were awful. In his view, *Danny* was ruined by poor casting since 'Jeremy Irons, as Danny's Dad is a splendid actor . . . but completely wrong for the part.' The television-cartoon version of his beloved BFG, on the other hand, was ruined 'by poor animation', but *The Witches*, according to Dahl, was 'the worst of the lot'.

This was all the more disappointing because it had a big budget, a top director in Nicolas Roeg, and two actresses he greatly admired: Anjelica Huston and Mai Zetterling. He first realized how wrong the enterprise was going at an early preview. Here's how Liccy Dahl describes what happened:

'We were sent for to watch some rushes and to see the ending. So over we went to sit in a small room with a movieola and tiny screen. There was Roald, myself,

Nick Roeg and one of the producers . . . and they put the ending on with Mai Zetterling playing the Grandmother magnificently. It was the true ending of the book and it was fantastic. Roald actually *cried*. He said 'Wonderful . . . wonderful'. Then Nick Roeg said 'Well, I have to show you something else. We have another ending.' And he left the room rather quickly and they put on this second, dreadful ending with the White Witch and the child where he turns back from a mouse to a little boy. And that, of course, was the version they chose. They lost the entire message of the book which is on its last page — that if someone really loves you it doesn't matter how you look, especially since Grandma and the boy-mouse would now die together. This was completely gone. Roald was devastated. Also, having sold the story to the studio already, he could do nothing whatever about it.'

Such, all too often, is the fate of writers when their work is transferred to the screen. Have we seen the last of Dahl in the cinema, then? This seems unlikely . . . already there's talk of a new movie, *James and the Giant Peach*, to be made by the Walt Disney Corporation. Roald Dahl will never see it, of course, but will his fans have better luck with this project?

Let's hope so.

6

Some Questions Answered

Children wrote to Roald Dahl from all over the world. They sent him letters, stories, scrapbooks, pictures, posters, poems — usually based on some aspect of his work that had caught their fancy. He always tried to answer every letter.

At Gipsy House there was a small but fully-equipped office and each morning at 9.30 Roald's secretary would come in and take dictation. 'Every week or so she says we need a new letter for teachers,' he told me. 'They frame them, stick them on noticeboards and give each child a copy to take home. We never say 'Dear Miss Thingy'. We put, 'Lovely, gorgeous Sheila and all the clever children in your class.' So there's always a giggle.'

Much less welcome were the visits from uninvited trippers with cameras who used to wait at Roald Dahl's garden gate. 'I try to ignore them. Theo will say, 'There's some here again,' and I maybe hover trying not to walk across the garden to the hut, but I mostly just carry on and do go. I suppose I don't mind really.'

Many of the questions children used to ask him in their letters have been answered in earlier chapters. Here are some others which cropped up most often.

Meeting Princess Margaret at the opening of *Willy Wonka and the Chocolate Factory* — a screen version of *Charlie* heartily disliked by its author

Where Does a Writer Get His Ideas?

Someone once asked this of the great Russian composer Stravinsky — thinking he would reply 'When I'm walking in the woods' or perhaps 'While I'm staring at my shaving mirror'. Instead he answered 'At the piano'. Roald Dahl loved this story because it emphasized that ideas don't just happen, they must be *made* to happen through hard work. 'You start with the germ of an idea,' he insisted, 'a tiny little germ ... a chocolate factory? Suddenly you know it's going to fascinate children and you build round that. Or on that tree there — a peach ... a peach that goes on growing — not the size of those ones, a peach that just doesn't stop growing. You never see the whole landscape of the story. You work it out

64

and play around with it. You doodle . . . you make notes . . . it grows, it grows . . .'

Occasionally, though, a good idea would flit into his mind when he wasn't in his hut. When this occurred he'd rush for a pencil, a crayon, a lipstick, anything that would write, and 'scribble a few words that will later remind me of the idea. Often, one word is enough.' Once he returned home, Dahl was careful to transfer the idea to an old red-covered school exercise book he had owned for almost forty years. This precious notebook only gave him a starting-point, however, since any story 'builds and expands while you are writing it. All the best stuff comes at the desk'.

Which is Harder — Writing for Adults or Writing for Children?

Roald Dahl had few doubts about this. 'Writing for children is harder than writing for adults . . . children don't have the concentration of adults and unless you hold them from the first page, they're going to wander away and watch the telly or do something else. They only read for fun; you've got to hold them.' He backed up this opinion with a true story about the American publishers Crowell-Collier who about twenty years ago wrote to all the leading writers for adults at that time offering each of them an enormous sum of money — 'five or ten thousand dollars, I think it was' — to write a short story for children. The intention was to make this the best ever collection of tales for young people. Alas, the project soon had to be abandoned because only one

From *Esio Trot* (© Quentin Blake, 1990, Jonathan Cape)

of the stories sent in was good enough. Two years later
it was published on its own. It was called *The Magic
Finger* — by Roald Dahl.

There are very few authors who consistently write for
children and adults, as Dahl did. And even fewer can

write for children of different ages. Roald Dahl may well be unique in having produced successful books for just about every age-group from toddlers to teenagers and beyond: *The Giraffe and the Pelly and Me* (4–5 years), *Fantastic Mr Fox* (5–6 years), *Charlie* and *Esio Trot* (7–8 years), *Matilda* (8–10 years) and *Henry Sugar* for those who are 'no longer children and have not yet become adults'.

What was so special about Roald Dahl that enabled him to do this?

My guess is that there were two reasons. Firstly, he had a marvellous ability to pinpoint a specific audience and to 'impersonate' it exactly. When asked how he could communicate so readily with eight-year-olds he once replied, 'I *am* eight years old'. And so he was — or five or ten or fifteen years old, as necessary. Secondly, he wrote with the same sharpness, directness and refusal to waste words whatever the age of his readers. Compare, for example, his children's story *Danny The Champion of the World* with the adult story on which he based it — 'The Champion of the World' from his collection *Kiss, Kiss*. Each has whole passages that would fit the other perfectly without a word being changed. The chief difference between the two is that of viewpoint. One of Roald Dahl's great strengths consisted in not dressing his language up when he wrote for adults and not scaling it down when he wrote for children.

Which is Roald Dahl's Best Book?

This is an impossible question to answer. You must

decide for yourself which has the most thrilling story, uses the most exciting language, is the most *fun*. Remember that your opinion about this may well alter as you read your next Dahl book or re-read an earlier one. Even the world's greatest critics of the world's greatest books have sometimes changed their minds.

Which Book Did Roald Dahl Think Was His Best?

The BFG.

And he was right, of course ... or was he? This will depend on your answer to the previous question!

What Sort of A Person Must I Be To Become An Author?

This question was answered by Roald Dahl in his article 'Lucky Break' which is included in *The Wonderful Story of Henry Sugar*:

1. You should have a lively imagination.
2. You should be able to write well. By that I mean you should be able to make a scene come alive in the reader's mind. Not everybody has this ability. It is a gift, and you either have it or you don't.
3. You must have stamina. In other words, you must be able to stick to what you are doing and never give up, for hour after hour, day after day, week after week and month after month.
4. You must be a perfectionist. That means you must never be satisfied with what you have written until you have re-written it again and again, making it as good as you possibly can.

From *The BFG* (© Quentin Blake 1982)

5. You must have strong self-discipline. You are working alone. No one is employing you. No one is around to give you the sack if you don't turn up for work, or to tick you off if you start slacking.

6. It helps a lot if you have a keen sense of humour. This is not essential when writing for grown-ups, but for children it's vital.

7. You must have a degree of humility. The writer who

thinks that his work is marvellous is heading for trouble.

Do you have the qualities on this list? Since you've been interested enough to read this far then the chances are you've got at least some of them. Few writers are as successful as Roald Dahl was, remember. But some people might have been if only they'd risked their *time* by keeping that bum on a chair when it was the last thing they felt like doing. It's the biggest gamble of all.

Who is Roald Dahl's best illustrator?

As you'd expect, during his long career Roald Dahl was teamed with a number of top illustrators — including Jill Bennett, Patrick Benson, Faith Jacques and Michael Foreman.

Roald himself had no doubt about his preference, though: Quentin Blake. 'It is Quent's pictures rather than my own written descriptions that have brought to life such characters as the BFG, Miss Trunchbull, Mr Twit and the Grand High Witch ... when he and I work together on a new book and he has a pen in his hand, it is magical to watch the facility with which he can sketch a character or scene.'

How many Quentin Blake illustrations can you spot in this book? You'll find pictures of at least two of the characters mentioned above along with examples from other Dahl illustrators to help you decide your own favourite.

Finally, here's one last question:

Does Roald Dahl Have a Fan Club I Could Join?

Not quite a Fan Club, no. But, his publishers — Jonathan Cape in hardback and Puffin in paperback — do issue The Roald Dahl Newsletter from time to time. This can be obtained from Random House Children's Books, 20 Vauxhall Bridge Road, London SW1V 2SA. Announced in Newsletter 5 was The Roald Dahl Foundation which Liccy Dahl launched in the Autumn of 1992 with a spectacular concert at London's Royal Festival Hall. Included in the programme was Paul Patterson's musical setting of 'Little Red Riding Hood' which the Foundation hopes will become as popular on disc and cassette as Roald's *Revolting Rhymes* are on the page.

The aims of the Roald Dahl Foundation are to raise money to help three different problems: reading and writing (literacy), blood disorders (haematology) and head and spinal injuries (neurology). How can you help? Liccy Dahl suggests 'by organizing unusual events for raising funds (with a little help from your parents and teachers!), by spreading the word about the Foundation ... and by trying to get to one of the Concerts when it comes to your area'.

For full details write to Gipsy House, Great Missenden, Buckinghamshire, which you visited in Chapter Two of this book.

7

How Good a Children's Writer Was Roald Dahl?

This may seem a strange question to ask. If the world's young readers were invited to vote for their favourite author, wouldn't Roald Dahl come out well in front?

That's exactly the problem for some adult critics. They argue that the only way for a writer to build up Roald Dahl's vast following is to pander to the *worst* side of children, to appeal to those parts of every youngster which are cruel, grabby and easily satisfied. Yes, I agree this is nonsense — not to mention insulting. Nevertheless, it's a sad fact that Roald Dahl had to wait many years for his achievement to be 'officially' recognized. Britain's top prizes for children's literature usually went to other writers. Here, too, he was something of an outsider.

Until the spring of 1983, that is. This was when *The BFG* won the third Children's Book Award which is given by the Federation of Children's Book Groups. The award is unusual in that children themselves actually play a part in deciding who should win — or have the last word when it comes to the final choice.

The award co-ordinator was Pat Thomson who reported that, '*The BFG* has a particular language of his own and the children enjoyed the amazing

Signing autographs in a bookshop

vocabulary and the giant lore ... it combined many of the features that make a book work for children: an exciting beginning, humour at their level and striking memorable characters'. Such praise will come as no surprise to you, of course. It's only adult critics who can be so slow on the uptake. Nevertheless even grown-ups get it right eventually and after this, as we've seen, Roald Dahl's achievement in persuading young readers all over the world that books can be *fun* began to get the credit it deserved.

Even so, there are still plenty of grown-ups who rather regret his continuing popularity. This is a good reason for letting everyone know just why you like his work: firstly, as a reminder that children's books belong to *children* and not to the grown-ups who — strictly for your own good as usual — would like them to be as much like adult books as possible; secondly, to encourage more writers to develop skills that match his. After all, if it were that simple to 'Do-A-Dahl' wouldn't umpteen authors have caught up with him by now?

So what good arguments can be offered in favour of Dahl's work?

Plenty, but it's better for you to come up with these on your own than for me to do your thinking for you. In other words you must become a critic yourself. This is easier than you might think provided you never forget that the main purpose of literature is *enjoyment*. Though some authors, in some books (Roald Dahl included) may also set out to inform, or to enlighten, or to make a moral point, the over-riding aim of all stories is to *entertain*. The critic's job is to increase our fun by helping us understand if and why and how this entertainment works. In my view Roald Dahl's flair and craftsmanship and feel for his audience stand up well to the closest critical scrutiny. So how should you go about proving this?

First you must decide what and who you're comparing him *with*. For example, how does he rate for entertainment-value with your other favourite amusements — comics, television, video-games or cinema? In what ways does he mimic their storytelling methods?

How far does he match their instant impact, their zest, their jokes and their sparkiness? I ask this on behalf of teachers everywhere who give thanks to Roald Dahl almost daily for writing stories that don't assume every child is a natural bookworm.

Second, compare different Dahl stories. Are they equally exciting? Equally funny? If so, what are they getting right? If not, what's gone wrong? Try looking for themes that crop up in several books — revenge, for instance. Is it always handled in the same way? Remember that an author can develop his skills book by book ... also that it's rare for a writer to be on top form all the time.

Third, put Dahl's stories alongside those of one of the few authors who can match him in popularity: Enid Blyton. In persuading children to keep on turning over the pages, she's probably his equal. But in every other respect, I'd suggest, he's in a different class. Compare especially their approach to the following:

1. Storytelling

   Do her tales stick in the memory with the same sharpness and quirkiness that his do? Is this a question of what's in the story or the way the story is told? Does one of them leave you wondering about what's right and wrong in life more than the other one does?

2. Humour

   Which makes you laugh more? Why? What about?

3. Language
   Try reading both authors aloud. Do they write with the same freshness and excitement? Is it easier to recall memorable scenes, or pieces of description, or even single words from one rather than from the other?

If you think hard about these matters then you'll discover more than enough evidence to explain your liking for Roald Dahl's work. Also you'll learn a lot about the sheer *skill* that's needed to write as well as he did. You may even be tempted to probe a little deeper and analyse one of his books in detail — that is, to take it apart to find out how it operates. For instance, you might focus on the plot of a Roald Dahl story to reveal the crafty way in which he reaches his famous slam-bam endings — as in *George's Marvellous Medicine,* where he sets the reader up for what finally happens to Grandma Kranky by having her complain in the very first chapter that growing is 'a nasty childish habit'. Or you could take a particular character such as Willy Wonka and examine his eerie presentation as both a young kid and an old codger. Another possibility for a sensitive critic is the teasing out of the way fact meets fiction in a story ... it's easy enough to identify Sophie in *The BFG* as Dahl's own grand-daughter since she also wears glasses with 'steel rims and very thick lenses'. But what about Sophie's mission to teach the Big Friendly Giant 'how to speak properly'. Doesn't this remind you of Roald's problem after Patricia Neal's stroke many years before?

From *The BFG* (© Quentin Blake 1982)

On a different subject altogether, you might compare the way he uses flight and flying, say, in tales he wrote at different times in his career — *The Magic Finger* at the beginning. 'The Swan' from *The Wonderful Story of Henry Sugar* in the middle, and *The Minpins* right at the end.

These are just some of the ways in which you can explore Roald Dahl's work. You'd better be careful though. The analytic approach does have one nasty drawback for a critic. If you dissect a story too much you may end up killing off all the fun of it. Always put the book back together again afterwards by re-reading it just for enjoyment. This is only fair to any author, but especially one like Roald Dahl who always insisted that 'the job of a children's writer is to try to write a book that is so exciting and fast and wonderful that the child falls in love with it'. It's a job he was marvellously good at, as the best reviewers have been quick to recognize.

Roald Dahl, The Champion of the World of Children's Books

When *Charlie and the Chocolate Factory* was first published, the critic Naomi Lewis spotted its quality straightaway: 'A real treat ... apart from some therapeutic treatment for the nasties there is nothing but pleasure in this dazzling book ... tension, magic, magnificent plot, scrumptious details, thrilling pictures ...' Millions of children agree with her. For them Roald Dahl himself is the Big Friendly Giant. In a newspaper interview he once remarked: 'I suppose I could knock at the door of any house where there was a child — whether it was the US, Britain, Holland, Germany, France — and say 'My car's run out of petrol. Could you please give me a cup of tea?' And they'd know me. That

78

does make me feel good.'

Who wouldn't have felt good about winning a readership like this? Could it be that Roald Dahl's books are so popular because they're the kind that children would write for each other if they had enough stamina and language experience? Do youngsters recognize at once that here was a writer who shares their relish for sharp contrasts, their liking for pace in a story, their preference for laughing out loud at each other, at grown-ups, at stuffiness in all its aspects?

You're in a better position to answer these questions than I am, of course, because he wrote for you, not me.

To Roald Dahl *your* opinion was always far more important than that of any critic — even one who tried hard to understand and appreciate his achievement. This is a rare compliment for an adult author to pay a young reader.

No wonder so many grown-ups find Roald Dahl's writing such a threat. And no wonder so many children still think of him as the Storytelling Champion of the World.

Roald Dahl's Books

For Adults

Over to You	1945
Someone Like You	1948
Sometime Never	1948
Kiss Kiss	1959
Switch Bitch	1965
My Uncle Oswald	1979
The Best of Roald Dahl	1983
Ah, Sweet Mystery of Life	1989
Memories with Food at Gipsy House	1991

For Adults and Children

Boy: Tales of Childhood	1984
Going Solo	1986
My Year	1993

For Children

The Gremlins	1944
James and the Giant Peach	1961
Charlie and the Chocolate Factory	1964
The Magic Finger	1966
Fantastic Mr Fox	1970
Charlie and the Great Glass Elevator	1973
Danny The Champion of the World	1975
The Wonderful Story of Henry Sugar	1977
The Enormous Crocodile	1978
The Twits	1980
George's Marvellous Medicine	1981
Revolting Rhymes	1982
The BFG	1982
The Witches	1983
Dirty Beasts	1984
Giraffe and the Pelly and Me	1985
Matilda	1988
Rhyme Stew	1989
Esio Trot	1990
The Vicar of Nibbleswicke	1991
The Minpins	1991